"Oh, to be a Vulcan"

Kamy Lynn Neumann

"Oh, to be a Vulcan"

Kamy Lynn Neumann

If you would like to contact Kamy or book her for speaking appointments then e-mail her at:
kamylynn@ymail.com

Published by *Neu Creation Ministry*
326 South 28th Avenue | Brighton CO 80601 USA

Published in the United States of America
Philosophy/Religion
ISBN: 978-1547054749

Neo-Stoicism

This book is dedicated to all the Stoic Philosophers of our day. May your journey be one of true happiness as you find the end is really just the beginning.

A.D. 2017

Introduction

The television series "Star Trek" that debuted in 1966 instantly captivated millions in the United States and around the globe. Who hasn't lain in bed at night and contemplated the vastness of space and the universe and wondered what lies beyond? Star Trek, a fictional long running series and movies about other worlds and extraterrestrials and their interaction and involvement with humanity has intrigued and entertained like no other. Why? Is it because the idea of discovering, studying and understanding others is often the very means by which we begin to understand ourselves? By reaching back or out or up we are pushed beyond what we perceive as our limits and little by little are shaped into what makes us who we are. Even fiction can hit pretty close to home when dealing with our own problems, tendencies and characteristics as human beings.

The question, "who am I?" is a question that has been asked and contemplated by most intelligent, thinking people for centuries including the well known Greek Philosophers of ancient times and in my opinion can ultimately only be answered by one source, the One who created all things. This is a book that delves into the Ancient Greek philosophy of Stoicism and its intertwining relationship with Christianity. I have found the belief and practice of Neo-Stoicism to be one of the most effective and useful tools to achieving ultimate happiness, peace and contentment as an imperfect human in a chaotic and sinful world. I must also say, however, that even while penning these words I am at the *present* time experiencing one of the most emotionally challenging and unstable experiences of my life. The expression "physician, heal thyself," is a very fitting one for me, indeed. In other words, sometimes no matter how logical, reasonable and life bettering one knows something to be doesn't always mean it's easy to put into practice. I am, after all, human and not a Vulcan which makes the successful practice of not being an emotionally driven person much easier said than done. Not only that but I am also a woman and even though I run the risk of being harshly criticized for this statement, I realize that as a woman, being emotionally driven can often come even more naturally to me. Perhaps that's why I have learned that it takes more than just a good ancient philosophy like Stoicism to be truly effective. What is the secret of actually putting this great philosophy into practice? We will begin our journey on the fictional planet of Vulcan and explore a metaphorical depiction of Stoicism in a make believe, albeit applicable way.

Chapter 1

"Oh, to be a Vulcan"

ho are Vulcan? For those who have never been interested in watching Star Trek, Vulcan are a fictional Extraterrestrial humanoid species in the Star Trek franchise who originate from the planet Vulcan. In the various Star Trek television series and movies they are noted for their attempt to live by logic and reason with no interference from emotion.

As my study into Stoicism progressed I realized they were the perfect example to use for my depiction. Just think; a whole planet of radical Stoic extremists!

The most famous and beloved of all the Vulcan is none other than Mr. Spock, Captain Kirk's side kick and first mate on the Starship Enterprise to "boldly go where no one has gone before..." Spock's character is an interesting study as he is actually half Human/ half Vulcan (on His Dad's side :).

Mr. Spock's character depicts a Vulcan who is resolutely dedicated to the Vulcan laws and practice. These fictional extraterrestrials are actually intrinsically very emotional to the point that they are even capable of being enraged enough to kill their own brother or closest friend (the story of Cain and Abel come to mind) and because of this dilemma of inherently strong emotions a wise and revered Vulcan named Surak came up with the code of emotional control: controlling emotions by suppression and choosing to be driven basically by nothing but logic and reason. This fictional depiction is not entirely made up. I believe Star Trek borrowed the philosophy of some of the Ancient Greeks to create the Vulcan race for their show. Seneca, who we will get better acquainted with through this book, was a well known Stoic philosopher. When asked to give his advice on quelling the emotion of anger here is some of what he had to say on the subject:

You have importuned me, Novatus, to write on the subject of how anger may be allayed, and it seems to me that you had good reason to fear in an especial degree this, the most hideous and frenzied of all the emotions. For the other emotions have in them some element of peace and calm, while this one is wholly violent and has its being in an onrush of resentment, raging with a most inhuman lust for weapons, blood, and punishment, giving no thought to itself if only it can hurt another, hurling itself upon the very point of the dagger, and eager for revenge though it may drag down the avenger along with it. Certain wise men, therefore, have claimed that anger is temporary madness. For it is equally devoid of self-control, forgetful of decency, unmindful of ties, persistent and diligent in whatever it begins, closed to reason and counsel, excited by trifling causes, unfit to discern the right and true — the very counterpart of a ruin that is shattered in pieces where it overwhelms. But you have only to behold the aspect of those possessed by anger to know that they are insane. For as the marks of a madman are unmistakable — a bold and threatening mien, a gloomy brow, a fierce expression, a hurried step, restless hands, an altered color, a quick and more violent breathing —

so likewise are the marks of the angry man; his eyes blaze and sparkle, his whole face is crimson with the blood that surges from the lowest depths of the heart, his lips quiver, his teeth are clenched, his hair bristles and stands on end, his breathing is forced and harsh, his joints crack from writhing, he groans and bellows, bursts out into speech with scarcely intelligible words, strikes his hands together continually, and stamps the ground with his feet; his whole body is excited and 'performs great angry threats'; it is an ugly and horrible picture of distorted and swollen frenzy — you cannot tell whether this vice is more execrable or more hideous. Other vices may be concealed and cherished in secret; anger shows itself openly and appears in the countenance, and the greater it is, the more visibly it boils forth...And yet I am aware that the other emotions as well are not easily concealed; that lust and fear and boldness all show their marks and can be recognized beforehand. For no violent agitation can take hold of the mind without affecting in some way the countenance. Where, then, lies the difference? In this — the other emotions show, anger stands out.

--Seneca To Novatus On Anger

Back to our metaphor; in Star Trek: The Original Series episode "Journey to Babel", Spock says that "Vulcan do not approve of violence", and that it is, "illogical to kill without reason". Here is another quote by a famous Stoic that backs up this line of thinking:

You shouldn't give circumstances the power to rouse anger, for they don't care at all.
--Marcus Aurelius. Meditations, 7.38

Moving from a fictional application to a non-fictional one from the Bible that goes back much further than even the Ancient Greeks, Had Cain (Adam and Eve's eldest son) not allowed his emotion of anger to control him and used a more logical and rational approach to dealing with his feelings toward his brother Abel, perhaps he would have made a different choice than killing his brother in a fit of rage and eventually would have realized that his own error in judgment, not his brother's obedience, was actually the culprit for his predicament of his worship and sacrifice not being acceptable to God. The Vulcan chose to take a very radical approach to solving the problem of being misled by their emotions by completely doing away with emotions for the most part. I do not believe this is the answer to our human problem on planet earth, as compassion and empathy would also become nonexistent, but there is sure some wisdom that can be gained from a less emotionally driven and more logically and rationally driven existence that would ultimately be a win/win for everyone.

As I sit here contemplating all I have gone through and the ways I have chosen to deal with problems and issues especially in relationships in my own 42 years of life on planet Earth, I realize that in a way, I wish I could somehow morph into a half breed Vulcan myself. By this I mean that I am realizing that life seems to be more balanced and easier to handle when I am able to repress my emotions, particularly the negative ones. Logic seems a much truer friend than emotions and much more stable, enabling me to accomplish my goals and purposes that I believe I was placed into this world for. I have actually experienced illness from my past emotional state at times that have proved to be extremely debilitating because feelings have a way of distorting things, sometimes in a seemingly good way by initiating a positive emotion, and sometimes in a bad or negative way. Whichever way it is, it does not usually produce a realistic or even a true picture of the situation making things appear better or worse than they really are. It is my goal to gain as much insight and wisdom as I can from the philosophy of controlling emotions through Stoicism and finding where the secret of actually being able to successfully practice it really lies.

Chapter 2

"Oh, to be a Stoic"

toicism was founded in Athens as a school of Hellenistic philosophy in the early 3rd century BC by Zeno of Citium. The basic philosophy of Stoicism is to achieve personal maturity and fulfillment by practicing ethics based on the laws of nature. For example, instead of remaining in a constant state of dissatisfaction and always wanting more, one should be satisfied with what you have been given and make the most of it. In addition one should be logical and rational and not carried away by passion and emotion. Stoicism flourished throughout the Roman and Greek world with some of the most complete written works on the philosophy accomplished by Lucius Annaeus Seneca whose assessment on the emotion of anger we read in the last chapter. He was a Roman Stoic philosopher and statesman who was an advisor to Emperor Nero. He was Born in 4 BC in Córdoba,

Spain and died in 65 AD in Rome, Italy. Considering Nero's bad reputation and extremely poor judgment I wonder at the lack of putting into practice the wisdom of his advisors, but a person can receive all the good advice in the world and choose not to take it. Seneca was actually a contemporary of Paul the Apostle who wrote most of the New Testament. Saul of Tarsus, who later, when converted, became Paul the Apostle of Jesus Christ, was born in 4 BC in Tarsus in Cilicia which is now in Turkey. Ironically Paul lived almost exactly the same time as Seneca as he died around 62–64 AD in Rome. There are quite a few examples of similarities in some of the well known quotes by Seneca as well as other well known Stoic philosophers and verses I've found in the writings of Paul in the New Testament. The evidence that Paul was not only acquainted with but also influenced by Stoic philosophy cannot be denied.

While Paul was waiting for them in Athens, he was greatly distressed to see that the city was full of idols. So he reasoned in the synagogue with both Jews and God-fearing Greeks, as well as in the marketplace day by day with those who happened to be there. A group of Epicurean and Stoic

philosophers began to debate with him.
 Acts 17:16-18

This fact has actually been a source of contention and criticism by atheists and those who would discount and reject Christianity. Here is an example of a quote by Seneca to compare with Paul's writings found in the New Testament Scriptures.

True happiness is to enjoy the present, without anxious dependence upon the future, not to amuse ourselves with either hopes or fears but to rest satisfied with what we have, which is sufficient, for he that is so wants nothing. The greatest blessings of mankind are within us and within our reach. A wise man is content with his lot, whatever it may be, without wishing for what he has not.
--Seneca

I am not saying this because I am in need, for I have learned to be content whatever the circumstances. I know what it is to be in need, and I know what it is to have plenty. I have learned the secret of being content in any and every situation, whether well fed or hungry, whether living in plenty or in want.
--Paul (Philippians 4:11-12 NIV)

There are actually many examples of a back and forth influence between the Scriptures and Stoic philosophers. Much of Stoicism was based on the idea that one can overcome negative and destructive emotions by suppressing and transforming them with self control and fortitude. This is accomplished by exercising one's mind with positive thinking and following it through by living a disciplined life of logic and reason based on ethics and moral values. For a Stoic, this was not just a belief but a way of life that involved both practice and training. Paul found this to be true when practicing true Christianity as well.

And every man that striveth for the mastery is temperate in all things. Now they do it to obtain a corruptible crown; but we an incorruptible. I therefore so run, not as uncertainly; so fight I, not as one that beateth the air: But I keep under my body, and bring it into subjection: lest that by any means, when I have preached to others, I myself should be a castaway.
--Paul (1 Corinthians 9:25-27 KJV)

Temperance, or self control was one of the four "cardinal virtues" taught by Plato; wisdom, courage and justice made up the other three. Stoicism first appeared in Athens around 300 years before Christ. Jesus taught many things that would have been agreed upon and understood by a Stoic philosopher. This is another point of contention for those who criticize Christianity. We will delve into this more later.

After Jesus accomplished His mission on earth and placed His disciples and apostles in charge of spreading the gospel, many Greeks were converted to Christianity. The philosophy of Stoicism found an even stronger foundation on which to base its practice as belief in Jesus and Christian principles seemed to blend naturally with the philosophy of Stoicism. This blend became known as Neo-Stoicism. A very good example of what was believed and practiced by both Stoics and Christians was sexual purity.

No longer was she merely the dancing-girl who extorts a cry of lust and concupiscence from an old man by the lascivious contortions of her body; who breaks the will, masters the mind of a King by the spectacle of her quivering bosoms, heaving belly and tossing thighs; she was now revealed in a sense as the symbolic incarnation of world-old Vice, the goddess of immortal Hysteria, the Curse of Beauty

supreme above all other beauties by the cataleptic
spasm that stirs her flesh and steels her muscles, - a
monstrous Beast of the Apocalypse, indifferent,
irresponsible, insensible, poisoning.
--Author: Joris Karl Huysmans

If I didn't know better I would believe the above quote to be a speech from one of the ancient Stoic philosophers, for this description of a dancing girl and her effect on men and the concluding remarks would have been something a Stoic would have agreed upon without question.

It is easier to exclude harmful passions than to rule
them, and to deny them admittance than to control
them after they have been admitted.
--Seneca

Passion was something the Stoic was very vary of and purposely tried to avoid, for it was seen as a terrible weakness and way to be controlled by something or someone else. Many Stoics found that excluding the erotic relationships was a good way to stay in control of one's own life. Even Paul found this to be pretty good advice.

Now to the unmarried and the widows I say: It is good for them to stay unmarried, as I do. But if they cannot control themselves, they should marry, for it is better to marry than to burn with passion.
--Paul (1 Corinthians 7:8-9 NIV)

He explains in an earlier verse that when you are married you lose some of your rights to yourself and must consider another person when making decisions.

The wife does not have authority over her own body but yields it to her husband. In the same way, the husband does not have authority over his own body but yields it to his wife.
--Paul (1 Corinthians 7:4 NIV)

I have to laugh a little at the idea of everyone taking this wise old advice as none of us would be here. I want to be fair to Paul though. I think he did believe in the institution of marriage as a good thing for most people as he advised:

Marriage should be honored by all, and the marriage bed kept pure, for God will judge the adulterer and all the sexually immoral.
--Paul (Hebrews 13:4 NIV)

Learning to control one's passions is something both the Stoic and the Bible stresses. There is a problem however, and that is the condition of the carnal nature of man is rather powerless over passion. Seneca and Paul (to a degree) thought the easiest way to solve the problem is to just avoid it altogether instead of running the risk of falling prey to being conquered. However, it was God who created marriage in the first place and who made Eve a beautiful, enchanting creature for Adam to love and enjoy. It is the abuse of this erotic love that is the real problem by not knowing how to put it into its proper sphere and allowing passion towards even your spouse to override everything else, especially your duty to God.

It is God's will that you should be sanctified: that you should avoid sexual immorality; that each of you should learn to control your own body in a way that is holy and honorable, not in passionate lust... For God did not call us to be impure, but to live a holy life. Therefore, anyone who rejects this instruction does not reject a human being but God, the very God who gives you his Holy Spirit.
-Paul (1 Thessalonians 4:3-5,7,8 NIV)

So, why is it that a person can't solve the problem of sexual lust by getting married? I mean, lust shouldn't be a problem if the sexual desires can be satisfied with one's spouse, right? Wrong! Being married has never and never will solve the problem of uncontrolled passion. Instead, a bigger problem arises which is an even more serious vice, called adultery. Here's what Seneca had to say about adultery. Compare it to Jesus' teaching on the subject.

If a man lies with his wife as if she is another man's wife, he is an adulterer, though she will not be an adulteress.
--Seneca, On Firmness, vii.

Ye have heard that it was said by them of old time, Thou shalt not commit adultery: But I say unto you, That whosoever looketh on a woman to lust after her hath committed adultery with her already in his heart.
--Jesus (Matthew 5:27-28 KJV)

Talk about raising the bar on personal ethics and morals! A very different philosophy is being taught and encouraged in society today. It is considered perfectly acceptable to fantasize through imagination, movies, role play, etcetera, about someone other than your spouse in order to spice up the romance in your marriage. There are always those who will continue to push the boundaries further and further, justifying where the line is drawn once the line of morality is crossed. People often do not stop with fantasizing. Other vices become accepted even in a marriage because the new eventually becomes old or like the old saying, "familiarity breeds contempt," so people become desperate to satisfy the lust of the carnal nature which truthfully can never be quenched by this type of method.

Seneca's opinion on adultery is interesting since as a Greek he was not held to the standard of God's law by his people. However, he could have easily been acquainted with and influenced by the Mosaic Law found in Exodus 20 as well as Jesus and His teachings. The idea that one is actually responsible for one's thoughts as well as actions is something almost wholly ignored in the world. To personally judge one's own thoughts is to rise to a level of integrity that must be measured by something more than the carnal nature and judged by something outside of mere human standards. Charles Spurgeon said, "You cannot grow in grace to any high degree while you are conformed to the world." What makes up a person's character begins in the mind. My words and actions are manifestations of my thoughts. If my thoughts are in check I will have no trouble controlling the rest.

For the word of God is alive and active. Sharper than any double-edged sword, it penetrates even to dividing soul and spirit, joints and marrow; it judges the thoughts and attitudes of the heart. Nothing in all creation is hidden from God's sight. Everything is uncovered and laid bare before the eyes of him to whom we must give account.
--Paul (Hebrews 4:12-13 NIV)

The intrinsic element that Christianity added to the belief of living a good life and not yielding to the carnal nature was that it could only be successively done by submitting one's self to God as we find taught by the New Testament writers, like James:

Submit yourselves therefore to God. Resist the devil, and he will flee from you.
James 4:7 KJV

Many would argue with me and give examples of people they believe lived a successful Stoic existence without God. However, it is my belief that Stoicism on its own is the right goal but lacks the power to actually fully accomplish it. Even as a Christian with an understanding of God's moral law (knowing what I need to do) does not mean I have the ability to do it; this is because of the reality that as a human I am born a sinner with an inherent nature to do the opposite of what is good. After all:

Can an Ethiopian change his skin or a leopard its spots? Neither can you do good who are accustomed to doing evil.
Jeremiah 13:23 NIV.

The prophet Jeremiah also wrote,

The heart is deceitful above all things, and desperately wicked: who can know it?
Jeremiah 17:9 KJV.

Paul elaborates on this as well:

For when we were in the realm of the flesh, the sinful passions aroused by the law were at work in us, so that we bore fruit for death...At one time we too were foolish, disobedient, deceived and enslaved by all kinds of passions and pleasures. We

lived in malice and envy, being hated and hating one another.
--Paul (Romans 7:5 & Titus 3:3NIV)

Paul then explains the remedy to this seemingly hopeless problem:

But when the kindness and love of God our Savior appeared, he saved us, not because of righteous things we had done, but because of his mercy. He saved us through the washing of rebirth and renewal by the Holy Spirit, whom he poured out on us generously through Jesus Christ our Savior, so that, having been justified by his grace, we might become heirs having the hope of eternal life. This is a trustworthy saying. And I want you to stress these things, so that those who have trusted in God may be careful to devote themselves to doing what is good. These things are excellent and profitable for everyone.
Titus 3:4-8 NIV

The Bible as well as practical human experience teaches that it is God's grace that makes it possible to overcome the harmful passions of our nature.

For the grace of God has appeared that offers salvation to all people. It teaches us to say "No" to ungodliness and worldly passions, and to live self-controlled, upright and godly lives in this present age, while we wait for the blessed hope---the appearing of the glory of our great God and Savior, Jesus Christ, who gave himself for us to redeem us from all wickedness and to purify for himself a people that are his very own, eager to do what is good.
Titus 2:11-14 NIV

Jesus passion was self sacrifice. Human nature's passion is self gratification. Human emotion from a fallen nature will play into that every time and lead astray. Even some of the pagan, polytheistic Ancient Greeks understood this problem with being emotionally driven and controlled by passion. Until a perfect nature is possessed one must choose to be guided by logic, facts, and truth, not feeling.

We should, every night, call ourselves to an account: What infirmity have I mastered today? What passions opposed? What temptation resisted? What virtue acquired? Our vices will abate of themselves if they be brought every day to the shrift.
--Seneca

A person controlled by their passions is actually a slave. A quote by Edmund Burke expresses this:

Men of intemperate minds can never be free. Their passions forge their fetters.
--Edmund Burke: Appraisals and Evaluations. Edited by Daniel E. Ritchie. 1990. P.202

Neo-Stoicism takes the practically impossible and makes it absolutely attainable by simply adding Jesus Christ into the equation. It can be defined by what Paul explains in Galatians 5:24 NIV which states:

Those who belong to Christ Jesus have crucified the flesh with its passions and desires.

I believe the "Neo" in Stoicism is the secret key ingredient to living a happy, successful, virtuous life free from the enslavement of harmful passions. It is found in a life of temperance through the power of devotion to Jesus Christ and a reliance and submission on His Spirit and His Word. It actually requires a death to self experience followed by a rebirth experience. This is a daily choice, even a moment by moment decision that I have the power to make.

I find then a law, that, when I would do good, evil is present with me. For I delight in the law of God after the inward man: But I see another law in my members, warring against the law of my mind, and bringing me into captivity to the law of sin which is in my members. O wretched man that I am! Who shall deliver me from the body of this death? I thank God through Jesus Christ our Lord.
--Paul (Romans 7:21-25 KJV)

And why stand we in jeopardy every hour? I protest by your rejoicing which I have in Christ Jesus our Lord, I die daily.
--Paul (I Corinthians 15:30, 31 KJV)

Jesus answered and said unto him, 'Verily, verily, I say unto thee, except a man be born again, he cannot see the kingdom of God.
--Jesus (John 3:3 KJV)

Chapter 3

"Oh, to be like Jesus"

W e started our journey from the fictional analogy of the Vulcan to the nonfictional wisdom of the Stoics. We now explore the embodiment of a perfect example of true virtue: Jesus Christ, who was fully God and fully man. In Him we find a perfect balance, control and use of emotion to either express His depth of feeling or accomplish a logical goal instead of just reacting to the people and events happening around him. Let us use for example the story of Jesus found in John 2:13-17 NIV:

When it was almost time for the Jewish Passover, Jesus went up to Jerusalem. In the temple courts he found people selling cattle, sheep and doves, and others sitting at tables exchanging money. So he made a whip out of cords, and drove all from the temple courts, both sheep and cattle; he scattered the coins of the money changers and overturned their tables. To those who sold doves he said, "Get these out of here! Stop turning my Father's house into a market!" His disciples remembered that it is written: "Zeal for your house will consume me."

Jesus "zeal" may have appeared like anger when He cleared the temple but He was in reality in complete control and used His righteous indignation to make a point. Whereas, during His trial He seemed almost emotionless and without feeling as He faced His accusers, torture and ultimate death.

When he was accused by the chief priests and the elders, he gave no answer. Then Pilate asked him, "Don't you hear the testimony they are bringing against you?" But Jesus made no reply, not even to a single charge—to the great amazement of the governor.
Matthew 27:12-14 NIV

Before Jesus was arrested He had to face the ultimate emotional battle. We find the depiction of His struggle in Matthew 26:36-38 NIV:

Then Jesus went with his disciples to a place called Gethsemane, and he said to them, "Sit here while I go over there and pray." He took Peter and the two sons of Zebedee along with him, and he began to be sorrowful and troubled. Then he said to them, "My soul is overwhelmed with sorrow to the point of death. Stay here and keep watch with me."

The emotion of fear that Jesus was experiencing in the Garden of Gethsemane was perfectly understandable but had he given in, fear would have served no purpose but would have in fact kept Him from being able to accomplish His ultimate goal. He overcame fear through prayer and submission and resigned Himself to logic and the reason for all the apparent chaos which was His mission: to pay the price for Humanity and make a way for their salvation. Giving into emotions like fear and anger only weaken and debilitate, whereas reactions of logic and reason based on facts and truth develop resolve to strengthen and subdue negative emotions. I want to emphasize this aspect of Jesus control over fear because I think is one of the most important factors in being able to live a truly happy and worry free existence. Jesus instructs us:

Therefore I tell you, do not worry about your life.
Matthew 6:25 NIV

Therefore do not worry about tomorrow, for tomorrow will worry about itself. Each day has enough trouble of its own.
Matthew 6:34 NIV

Below are some quotes taken from a letter Seneca wrote to his friend Lucilius where he gives him some sound Stoic advice to consider:

There are more things, Lucilius, likely to frighten us than there are to crush us; we suffer more often in imagination than in reality...What I advise you to do is, not to be unhappy before the crisis comes; since it may be that the dangers before which you paled as if they were threatening you, will never come upon you; they certainly have not yet come. Accordingly, some things torment us more than they ought; some torment us before they ought; and some torment us when they ought not to torment us at all. We are in the habit of exaggerating, or imagining, or anticipating, sorrow...How often has the unexpected happened! How often has the expected never come to pass! And even though it is ordained to be, what does it avail to run out to meet your suffering? You will suffer soon enough, when it arrives; so look forward meanwhile to better things. What shall you gain by doing this? Time. There will be many happenings meanwhile which will serve to postpone, or end, or pass on to another person, the trials which are near or even in your very presence...But life is not worth living, and there is no limit to our sorrows, if we indulge our fears to the greatest possible extent...You yourself must say. "Well, what if it does happen? Let us see who wins!"

--Seneca Letters from a Stoic

Fear is an emotion that only came into being after man sinned and realized the consequences of sin, namely, death. Though it has its place, for the most part this emotion in particular is very destructive and debilitating because it blinds a person from seeing the potential solution and focuses entirely on the worst case scenario. It blocks the ability to use a logical and rational thought process. Fear is an emotion that would be best suppressed almost entirely. It is only useful to create caution and inhibition for youth and inexperience, once wisdom has been developed there is no longer any need for fear. Whether it be fear or any other emotion, for a sinful nature, uncontrolled emotion is dangerous because of the inclination toward evil. Here is what Paul has to say regarding fear:

For God hath not given us the spirit of fear; but of power, and of love, and of a sound mind.
2 Timothy 1:7 KJV

I mentioned in earlier chapters the controversy of Christianity with many modern day practitioners of Stoicism. There are those who try and prove that Christianity is nothing more than building on a foundation of Stoic philosophy; that Jesus is just an egocentric figure that was far less superior in wisdom than the pagan Stoic philosophers of the past but I would like to pose the age old question of what came first the chicken or the egg? If Jesus is God, the I Am before Abraham was, than it was He who was inspiring the Stoic philosophy in the first place and teaching through His own Spirit the wisdom that any human being came up with. Seneca believed this to be true himself:

God is near you, he is with you, he is within you. This is what I mean Lucillius: a Holy Spirit indwells within us, one who marks our good and bad deeds, and is our guardian. As we treat this spirit so are we treated by it. Indeed, no man can be good without the help of God. Can one rise to superior of fortune unless God helps him to rise? --Seneca, epistle 41.

Seneca understood a fundamental principle regarding the ability of a mortal to be able to fully put into practice what one believes. Jesus did not borrow the wisdom of the Stoic if He truly is God. Rather He was the originator of all the partially understood wisdom that they had and made it more fully comprehended in the manifestation of His life and sacrifice for mankind. He gave the gift of Himself in a fuller sense to show who God is and His plan for mankind and the possibility of eternity with God through belief in His Son and the gift of salvation. Sure, if Stoicism on its own could be successfully practiced it could be very beneficial for a happier and more content existence without adding Jesus into the equation; however, there is no hope of anything after this life. If an eternal existence is nothing more than a naive disillusionment than does it matter? But, if Jesus is who He and the Bible claims Him to be and life eternal with God is a possible reality than being simply a Stoic falls far short of what the Creator really has in mind for the human race.

Solomon, (who lived long before any Stoic philosopher) surmised:

All things are wearisome, more than one can say. The eye never has enough of seeing, nor the ear its fill of hearing. What has been will be again, what has been done will be done again; there is nothing new under the sun. Is there anything of which one can say, "Look! This is something new'? It was here already, long ago; it was here before our time."
--Solomon (Ecclesiastes 1:8-10 NIV)

So the ancient pagan Greek philosophers cannot really take credit for the idea of living a well disciplined, moral and virtuous life when we have even more ancient manuscripts and preserved writings of the Old Testament saying the same thing only given by inspiration of God to His chosen prophets and writers. If one wants to be honest about the origination of Stoic wisdom, one need look no further than the Old Testament of the Bible. There you will find just as many similar ideas for the Stoic philosophy as you find in the New Testament. Like this wise quote from Cato. Notice the similarity to Solomon's words:

I begin to speak only when I'm certain what I'll say isn't better left unsaid.
 --Cato

To everything there is a season, and a time to every purpose under the heaven...a time to keep silence, and a time to speak.
--Solomon Ecclesiastes 3:1,7 KJV

The underlying problem with atheists is they hate to give credit where credit is due or to admit that there really is a God and Creator that everyone, including themselves will one day be accountable to. In the end rebellion and denial of the truth will prove to be a loss of an infinite nature.

Chapter 4

"Oh to be a Happy Me"

Don't explain your philosophy. Embody it.
--Epictetus

It is kind of funny for me to use the above quote when I have just written a little book explaining my philosophy :).

I want to open this closing chapter with a question. What good is all the good advice and wisdom in the world if it is not put into practice in one's life? I want to encourage anyone reading this book to consider a Neo-Stoic lifestyle by choosing a well balanced, logic based existence instead of paralogizing your life with assumptions and being blown and tossed about by waves of changing, unstable emotions and unrealistic expectations. I often wonder if we, in our modern, more technologically advanced society with our so called "progressive" inclusiveness which often leads to embracing immorality and vice are also progressing in happiness? Or would it be worthwhile taking the time to go back and study the old paths and heed the wisdom of those who have gone before and seeing if there is anything to be gleaned and utilized by me as an individual in a modern society? Answering that question is pretty easy for me as I do not know very many truly happy or well balanced people who choose to live by common worldly philosophies. When I look around I see dissatisfaction, greed, selfishness, depression, emptiness and fear to a large degree. I would like to present 6 principles found in Philippians 4:8 and expounded on from a Stoic perspective. I believe practicing these principles will lead to true and fulfilling happiness as they are not dependent on what one possesses in a materialistic sense.

Wealth consists not in having great possessions, but in having few wants.
--Epictetus

Neither is it based on outward experiences or conditions.

You have power over your mind – not outside events. Realize this, and you will find strength.
--Marcus Aurelius

These are principles that are understood and practiced in the mind and lived out in the choices one makes each and every day. If these 6 principles are put into practice through the power of the Holy Spirit, I guarantee they will change your life and outlook in a very positive way and bring you peace, happiness and success in everything you do.

Your mind will take the shape of what you frequently hold in thought, for the human spirit is colored by such impressions.
--Marcus Aurelius

Principle #1: ~Whatsoever things are true~

For what does reason purport to do? 'Establish what is true, eliminate what is false and suspend judgment in doubtful cases.' ... What else does reason prescribe? "To accept the consequence of what has been admitted to be correct.
--Epictetus

You cannot practice Neo-Stoicism and be a relevant thinker. In other words truth is not based on one's own perspective or biased reasoning. I remember hearing the notion that truth is relative while as a young girl watching "Return of the Jedi" another space movie, where a Jedi master was explaining his interpretation of "truth" to his apprentice. He (Obi-Wan) told him:

"Luke, you're going to find that many of the truths we cling to depend greatly on our own point of view."

This is a very popular philosophy that has become the overriding principle used by most human beings today. Whatever I want to believe is truth to me even if it's not to you. But if this is the philosophy I choose to live by then virtually I make up my own moral code and decide for myself what is right and wrong, good or bad. And how will I decide this? When it's all boiled down it will be based on how I feel or my emotional state. If everyone did this there would be complete anarchy and no one would be free at all! If what I feel is the deciding factor than facts and reality are overlooked because each person would determine truth from their own biased perspective irrespective of anyone else's feelings or rights which are protected in God's moral law. If I believe there is no such thing as sin or absolute truth then I have no need for a Savior because I don't need to be saved from my natural inclinations or be forgiven if I believe what I feel is not wrong. My husband often paraphrases the quote, "Everyone is entitled to his own opinion but not his own facts."*Daniel Patrick Moynihan, U.S. Ambassador, Administration Official & Academic* by saying:

You can have your own belief but you can't have your own facts.

The evidence of cause and effect in practical real life experience backs up the Bible, which shows that the natural inclination of fallen man is sinful and is not going to lead me to true happiness let alone eternity with God.

The heart is deceitful above all things, and desperately wicked: who can know it?
Jeremiah 17:9 KJV

The example we are given by those in positions of influence and power, the politicians, the Hollywood stars and wealthy of the world are by in large unfortunately lacking when it comes to leading temperate, well balanced, happy lives. We see instead a childish, selfish nature whose lust for wealth, power and position almost rival the lust for base sexual indulgences and other addictions. We see an acceptance of wickedness and impurity to satisfy those who would shake off all restraint and responsibility to society and younger generations to follow. If the unrestrained life of passion is so much better than virtue then why does everyone seem so unfulfilled and miserable? Could it be that people are largely buying into a lie that they will somehow find the happiness they seek by giving into every inclination and desire of the moment? As stated at the beginning of this book, the truth about who we are and where happiness can be found is in only one source; our Creator and His Word which is only properly interpreted and understood through His Spirit. Everything else is simply a lie that leads to unhappiness and destruction.

In the beginning was the Word, and the Word was with God, and the Word was God. He was with God in the beginning. Through him all things were made; without him nothing was made that has been made. In him was life, and that life was the light of all mankind. The light shines in the darkness, and

the darkness has not overcome it...The true light that gives light to everyone was coming into the world. He was in the world, and though the world was made through him, the world did not recognize him. He came to that which was his own, but his own did not receive him. Yet to all who did receive him, to those who believed in his name, he gave the right to become children of God--- children born not of natural descent, nor of human decision or a husband's will, but born of God. The Word became flesh and made his dwelling among us. We have seen his glory, the glory of the one and only Son, who came from the Father, full of grace and truth.
John 1:1-5, 9-14 NIV

And this is the condemnation, that light is come into the world, and men loved darkness rather than light, because their deeds were evil. For every one that doeth evil hateth the light, neither cometh to the light, lest his deeds should be reproved. But he that doeth truth cometh to the light, that his deeds may be made manifest, that they are wrought in God.
John 3:19-21 KJV

Jesus answered, "I am the way and the truth and the life. No one comes to the Father except through me.
John 14:6 NIV

There is no room for various interpretations if one uses God and the Bible as the foundation of truth. There is simply one source and one way to that source, Jesus Christ.

Principle #2: ~Whatsoever things are honest~

If it is not right do not do it; if it is not true do not say it.
--Marc Aurelius, Meditations

What is the difference between truth and honesty? Truth is fact. It is reality based on what is verifiable evidence. This is why God sent His Son Jesus to this world. To give verifiable evidence of Himself and to truth which is also called light. Otherwise, we would have no way to know truth because anything not of God is darkness. Pilate asked Jesus a question that Jesus had already answered but Pilate did not want to accept.

You are a king, then!" said Pilate. Jesus answered,
"You say that I am a king. In fact, the reason I was
born and came into the world is to testify to the
truth. Everyone on the side of truth listens to me."
"What is truth?" retorted Pilate. With this he went
out again to the Jews gathered there and said, "I
find no basis for a charge against him.
John 18:37-38 NIV

Honesty is the result of the manifestation of
conviction. I become convinced that something is
true and I respond sincerely to my belief. Honesty is
not necessarily truth. One can be honest and sincere
and yet be wrong. Paul was very sincere as a
Pharisee and believed that he was right to kill Jesus'
followers. He had to be shown his error to realize
his sincerity was misplaced and to choose to be on
the side of what was really true.

I verily thought with myself, that I ought to do many
things contrary to the name of Jesus of Nazareth.
--Paul (Acts 26:9 KJV)

Paul could not decide for himself what was truth, he
recognized it when God showed him and chose to
surrender himself and what he had previously felt
was right and conform to the truth, to Jesus Christ.

Paul's sincerity was never in question, only what he thought was truth. So honesty must be accompanied by the sincere recognition and acceptance of truth.

Principle #3: ~Whatsoever things are just~

He who spares the wicked injures the good.
--Seneca

To be just is simply to be fair. There is no room for being biased or showing favoritism in true justice. I love the way the NIV puts it:

Do not follow the crowd in doing wrong. When you give testimony in a lawsuit, do not pervert justice by siding with the crowd, and do not show favoritism to a poor person in a lawsuit.
Exodus 23:2-3 NIV

As a compassionate human being I may feel sorry for someone less fortunate and want to give them allowances that I may not under other circumstances feel inclined to do. If I am truly a just person I will not allow my feelings (compassionate as they may be) to pervert my judgment. If I am entrusted with the duty of enacting laws or being a judge or a person who will in a greater or lesser degree decide a person's fate, when it comes to being just it is essential that I do not allow my emotions to override what is right. It is easy to side with those I sympathize with instead of basing my judgment on pure principles. The person I dislike may be the one who is right and who deserves to be treated fairly even though I may feel they don't deserve it. Making fair judgments and acting on unbiased facts regarding people and things is very important as society is largely shaped by the actions of a few who are in positions of trust. Their judgments are what make up the standards by which society functions. If their judgment is perverted and based on the feelings and sentiments of irrational thinking this can debilitate and weaken the moral fiber that protects and strengthens those living in a society.

Principle #4: ~Whatsoever things are pure~

It is not the incense, or the offering that is acceptable to God, but the purity and devotion of the worshipper.
--Seneca

Something that is pure in the spiritual sense is

untainted with evil. It is impossible to live in a world of sin and not be acquainted with it; however, I do not have to participate in evil things just because it is around me. I can choose to live by the grace of God and resist evil by submission to Him.

Submit yourselves, then, to God. Resist the devil, and he will flee from you. Come near to God and he will come near to you. Wash your hands, you sinners, and purify your hearts, you double-minded. James 4:7-8 NIV

For it is God who works in you to will and to act in order to fulfill his good purpose. Do everything without grumbling or arguing, so that you may become blameless and pure, "children of God without fault in a warped and crooked generation." Then you will shine among them like stars in the sky as you hold firmly to the word of life... Philippians 2:13-16 NIV

It takes a decided effort to keep one's mind pure from sinful thoughts.

Create in me a clean heart, O God; and renew a right spirit within me. Psalm 51:10 KJV

I choose what I think about, what I watch and what I listen to, to a great extent. Am I purposefully entertaining sin and vice by my choices?

For as he thinketh in his heart, so is he.
Proverbs 23:7 KJV

Principle #5: ~Whatsoever things are lovely~

Do not indulge in dreams of having what you have not, but reckon up the chief of the blessings you do possess, and then thankfully remember how you would crave for them if they were not yours.
--Marcus Aurelius, Meditations

The best way of curing self pity is to count your blessings. If I focus on the negative aspects of life I will inevitably be discouraged and disheartened. However, if I focus on the lovely aspects of life and all the blessings God has given me it will have a positive and enabling effect. Is the glass half empty or half full, so to speak? Am I thankful for the things I have and make the most of them, or do I grumble and complain until even what I have suddenly disappears? This lesson is expounded on by Jesus in Matthew 25:14 KJV

For the kingdom of heaven is as a man travelling into a far country, who called his own servants, and delivered unto them his goods. And unto one he gave five talents, to another two, and to another one; to every man according to his several ability; and straightway took his journey. Then he that had received the five talents went and traded with the same, and made them other five talents. And likewise he that had received two, he also gained other two. But he that had received one went and digged in the earth, and hid his lord's money. After a long time the lord of those servants cometh, and reckoneth with them. And so he that had received five talents came and brought other five talents, saying, Lord, thou deliveredst unto me five talents: behold, I have gained beside them five talents more. His lord said unto him, Well done, thou good and faithful servant: thou hast been faithful over a few things, I will make thee ruler over many things: enter thou into the joy of thy lord. He also that had received two talents came and said, Lord, thou deliveredst unto me two talents: behold, I have gained two other talents beside them. His lord said unto him, Well done, good and faithful servant; thou hast been faithful over a few things, I will make thee ruler over many things: enter thou into the joy of thy lord. Then he which had received the one talent came and said, Lord, I knew thee that thou art an hard man, reaping where thou hast not sown, and gathering where thou hast not strawed: And I was afraid, and went and hid thy talent in the earth: lo, there thou hast that is thine. His lord answered and said unto him, Thou wicked and slothful servant, thou knewest that I reap where I sowed not, and gather where I have not strawed: Thou oughtest therefore to have put my money to the exchangers, and then at my coming I should have received mine own with usury. Take therefore the talent from him, and give it unto him which hath ten talents. For unto every one that hath shall be given, and he shall have abundance: but from him that hath not shall be taken away even that which he hath.

It is ultimately my choice to give in to self pity and be led by the self gratifying philosophy of the world or to be thankful for who I am and what I have and make the most of it. How can I expect to be given more if I cannot do anything good with what I've already been given?

Principle #6: ~Whatsoever things are of good report~

A man thus grounded must, whether he wills or not, necessarily be attended by constant cheerfulness and a joy that is deep and issues from deep within, since he finds delight in his own resources, and desires no joys greater than his inner joys.
--Seneca

Good news is not usually what sells in societies on planet Earth. People have a way of being drawn to bad and tragic news and then wonder why they are so depressed. I made a choice to almost completely dispense with main stream media news when I became pregnant with my first child. Hearing biased and often misleading accounts about all the terrible and negative things going on led me into feelings of fear and depression as I was getting ready to bring a new life into such a disturbing and dangerous environment. Simply choosing to not expose myself to all the negativity helped a great deal in maintaining a positive outlook and being cheerful, as a result a very healthy and happy baby was born into the world and has made his own positive contribution to society and the people around him.

The very best and most overlooked news of all is the good news of the gospel, that God loves us and has a wonderful plan for the present as well as the future for everyone who believes and puts their trust in Him.

For I know the plans I have for you," declares the Lord, "plans to prosper you and not to harm you, plans to give you hope and a future.
Jeremiah 29:11 NIV

So what does Paul conclude regarding these 6 principles? They must be the overriding and continuous thoughts of our hearts and minds if we will ever be able to put them into practice.

If there be any virtue, and if there be any praise, think on these things.
Philippians 4:8 KJV

Living out the Stoic principles of virtue found in Philippians 4:8 is the best path to happiness on my journey through this life. Doing this successfully requires the supernatural power of the Holy Spirit living in me. What most people go through life not realizing is the power of the gift of choice that has been given to us by God. I decide my own destiny. I decide what kind of life I will live and the attitude that will accompany the circumstances that surround me with the exercise of my own mind:

And be renewed in the spirit of your mind; and that ye put on the new man, which after God is created in righteousness and true holiness.
Ephesians 4:23-24 KJV

A truly gratifying Neo-Stoic existence is possible. Becoming a new creature in Jesus Christ has been offered to the inherently depraved and sinful Human race. So, the only question that remains is, what path will I choose to take? Will it be the path that the majority on this planet chooses; a path described in lyrics to a song I recently heard?

Speak your mind, look out for yourself
The answer to it all is a life of wealth
Grab all you can cause you live just once
You got the right to do whatever you want
Don't worry about others or where you came from
It ain't what you were, it's what you have become
What have we become?
A self indulgent people
What have we become?
Tell me where are the righteous ones?
What have we become?
In a world degenerating
What have we become?
--D.C. Talk

Or, will I choose a path already mapped out by the virtuous, selfless life of Jesus and allow Him to be my guide and lead the way? Stoicism does not have to be nothing more than a "pie in the sky", unrealistic ancient Greek philosophy; a nice idea but completely out of reach for a human being. I am not a Vulcan but I was created in God's image with the potential to be what any Stoic would be proud of. In fact, even more, what Jesus Christ would be proud of. Will I make the decision to fulfill my ultimate purpose and reflect His image to the universe? I desire the path of virtue, what path do you choose?

If virtue precede us every step will be safe.
--Seneca

Kamy Lynn and her husband Brian S. Neumann are both authors and international speakers. They have written books on a variety of topics including politics, religion and philosophy. They have recently created a series of character building stories for children entitled The Bo Bear Books. You can find their books at Amazon or thebookpatch.com.

Soul Provider Daily Devotional
By Kamy Lynn Neumann

Enigma
By Kamy Lynn Neumann

The Bo Bear Books (Series)
By Kamy Lynn Neumann
Illustrated by Brian S. Neumann

The White Elephant
By Brian S. Neumann

The Sanctuary Unveiled
By Brian S. Neumann

Shadow of Death
By Brian S. Neumann